ARE YOU IGNORING GOD'S CALLS?

ARE YOU IGNORING GOD'S CALLS?

YOU CAN GHOST HIM FOREVER...
BUT HE'LL NEVER HANG UP

Jose M. Azares

autógrafo

TULSA | GUADALAJARA

Are You Ignoring GOD's Calls?
© 2025 by Jose M. Azares

Published by Autógrafo Books
Tulsa, Oklahoma | Guadalajara, Mexico

ISBN   978-1-963127-43-0 (paperback)
          978-1-963127-44-7 (ebook)

Cover design by Gustavo Cruz.

Printed in the United States of America
28 27 26 25   1 2 3 4

For those who haven't picked up yet but know something's calling.
May these pages help you realize—
it's been GOD all along.

"Call to Me, and I will answer you, and show you great and mighty things, which you do not know."
— Jeremiah 33:3

"Behold, I stand at the door and knock. If anyone hears My voice and opens the door, I will come in to him and dine with him, and he with Me."
— Revelation 3:20

"When I called, you did not answer;
When I spoke, you did not hear."
—Isaiah 65:12

Contents

Introduction

Whether you've been a believer for years, you're just starting your walk with GOD, or you aren't sure you even believe in GOD, we all experience something stirring within us—a persistent voice calling to our hearts...

Calling us.

So many people don't realize that GOD is calling them—sometimes through their deepest desires, struggles, and even pain.

For years, GOD tried to reach me so many times, but I was too busy—chasing success, seeking love, trying to "find myself." Every time He called, I looked at the screen and pressed ***"Ignore Call."***

Back then, I didn't recognize it was Him.

I thought it was just noise—just another spam call.

Looking back, those "calls" came in many forms.

A quiet tug in my heart telling me that there had to be more.

A deep restlessness that success couldn't satisfy.

The conviction after a bad decision.

The feeling that I was drifting, even when life looked good on paper.

At the time, I didn't see any of that as GOD reaching out. I just thought I was tired, or stressed, or being dramatic. But now I know—those were the early calls...

Subtle. Persistent. Full of mercy.

We often ignore GOD, convinced we have life figured out. I didn't answer because I was chasing what the world told me mattered—success, money, control, recognition. I was chasing dreams that looked impressive on the outside but slowly wore down my soul.

That is, until the very things I was chasing humbled me. Opportunities fell through. Relationships started falling apart. Anxiety crept in behind closed doors.

My pursuits led me straight into pain, loss, and disappointment.

Then, suddenly, I longed for that call.

But here's what I didn't understand:

His calls weren't meant to pull me away from my pursuits and desires.

His calls weren't reminders of how I had messed up.

His calls weren't meant to inflict more pain.

He was calling to guide me through it all.

"A man's heart plans his way, but the Lord directs his steps." — Proverbs 16:9 (NKJV)

He placed pursuits and desires in my heart for a reason—but I was chasing them alone. He called because He knew I was hurting and feeling lost. He called because He felt my pain—just like any loving Father would.

He called not to interrupt my life, but to lovingly lead me through it.

And all He wanted to say was:

"You don't have to carry this alone—do it *with* Me, Son. I gave you this path on purpose."

"Commit everything you do to the Lord. Trust Him, and He will help you." — *Psalm 37:5 (NLT)*

Have you been ignoring GOD's calls?

This book isn't something I simply decided to write—it's something GOD commanded me to share. He spoke to me through Ezekiel 2:8–9:

"You shall speak My words to them, whether they hear or whether they refuse, for they are rebellious. But you, son of man, hear what I say to you. Do not be rebellious like that rebellious house; open your mouth and eat what I give you. Now when I looked, there was a hand stretched out to me, and behold, a scroll of a book was in it."

When He revealed this verse to me, I laughed in amazement.

He couldn't have been clearer.

GOD wanted me to share what it was like to live without Him—and what changed when I finally answered His calls. He called me and gave me that verse as confirmation to write this book. He even gave me the name for it.

By that point, I had ignored Him far too many times. And I realized something:

If I had trusted Him earlier, I would have avoided so much unnecessary pain. I also would have created many opportunities He wanted to place before me—including this book.

So before writing a single page, I wrote this introduction.

I wanted to allow GOD to speak—not just to me, but to you.

The story that follows is deeply personal. It's about how I spent years ignoring GOD and what happened when I finally started answering His calls. But this book isn't just about my journey. It's an invitation for you to reflect on yours.

Because what I discovered when I started saying "yes" wasn't just change; **it was transformation.**

When I finally stopped ignoring His calls, GOD became:

The **first** one I run to.

The **only** voice I trust completely.

The **One** who leads me, and whom I obey without questioning.

It's easy to ignore GOD's calls when we're distracted by our own plans, timelines, and goals. But after many unnecessary hardships, I finally realized:

He wasn't trying to take something from me. He was calling me to something greater than I had ever imagined.

And... He's calling you, too.

Will you answer now when He calls?

The beautiful thing about GOD—His grace and mercy—is that you can always call Him back. No matter how long you've ignored Him, no matter how many times you've declined...

He is still waiting.

No matter how long it's been. No matter how far you've gone.

He is desperate to hear from you—His beloved son, His cherished daughter.

Right now, I invite you to pause and pray this simple prayer:

"Father, I'm sorry for ignoring You. I want to hear Your call.

Please speak to me and lead me back to You."

Then, just speak from your heart. Any words will move Him.

Now, put down this book.

Let GOD call you back.

You'll know when it's Him. Just trust that He's near.

And when He does, when He speaks to your heart in the next few minutes, hours, days, or weeks—pick this book up again. Because what comes next will show you what happens when you finally say yes to Him.

It's not just a moment.

It's the beginning of a relationship that will change your life!

Chapter 1

Recognizing GOD's Number on Your Caller ID

When He calls you, it may show up as **"Unknown"** on the screen of your mind and heart.

But deep down, you'll know it's Him.

He calls when you need guidance, support, or strength.
He calls when you're facing challenges, hardships, or uncertainty.
He calls when it's time for you to walk away from something holding you back.

It's like seeing an **"Unknown Caller"** on your phone— you hesitate to answer, yet something inside urges you to pick up. But unlike a random phone call, this isn't curiosity pulling at you. It's His Holy Spirit within you asking you to answer!

The Holy Spirit is like a spiritual transmitter inside your soul—constantly tuning your heart to GOD. Through whispers of encouragement, nudges of conviction, and moments of peace, the Holy Spirit is your direct connection to GOD. And the more you grow in faith and trust, the sharper and clearer that connection becomes.

"And without faith, it is impossible to please God, because anyone who comes to Him must believe that He exists and that He rewards those who earnestly seek Him." — Hebrews 11:6 (NIV)

If you're new to faith or still unsure about GOD, you may struggle with the idea of the Holy Spirit, the Bible, or even Jesus Christ Himself. And that's okay—I'm not here to convince or convert you.

I'm here to plant a seed, just as someone once planted one in me.

A seed that, over time, has grown and produced the most beautiful fruits in my life.

"I am the vine; you are the branches. If you remain in Me and I in you, you will bear much fruit; apart from Me you can do nothing." — John 15:5 (NIV)

Besides planting a seed, I also want to help you recognize His calls—so you stop ignoring them.

Why should you stop ignoring them?

Because He loves you in ways you can't imagine—and in ways you may have never felt before.

"Love is patient, love is kind. It does not envy, it does not boast, it is not proud. It does not dishonor others, it is not self-seeking, it is not easily angered, it keeps no record of wrongs. Love does not delight in evil but rejoices with the truth. It always protects, always trusts, always hopes, always perseveres." — 1 Corinthians 13:4–7 (NIV)

GOD often calls us through people and circumstances. These are the ways He speaks to us first—whether or not we believe in Him yet.

How can you tell if it's Him?

Because His presence triggers the fruits of the Spirit within you:
love, joy, peace, patience, kindness, goodness, faithfulness, gentleness, and self-control. These are lasting feelings.

"But the fruit of the Spirit is love, joy, peace, forbearance, kindness, goodness, faithfulness, gentleness and self-control. Against such things there is no law."
— *Galatians 5:22–23 (NIV)*

Anything else is not from Him:
Infatuation, passion, lust, anger, despair, anxiety, selfishness, hatred, fleeting pleasures.

"The acts of the flesh are obvious: sexual immorality, impurity and debauchery; idolatry and witchcraft; hatred, discord, jealousy, fits of rage, selfish ambition, dissensions, factions and envy; drunkenness, orgies, and the like. I warn you, as I did before, that those who live like this will not inherit the kingdom of God."
— *Galatians 5:19–21 (NIV)*

So, the next time you sense an **"Unknown Call"** in your heart and mind, remember—it might be Him reaching out.

Whether you're feeling joy or struggling with hurt, anxiety, confusion, or discouragement, He's not calling to shame or pressure you.
He's calling to walk with you, to lead you, and to remind you that you were never meant to do life alone.

"I will instruct you and teach you in the way you should go; I will counsel you with My loving eye on you."
— *Psalm 32:8 (NIV)*

If you're unsure about it, that's okay. Many of us start in the same place, questioning what we can't see or fully understand. But the beauty of GOD's calls is that He meets us where we are, even in our doubt, weakness, fear, confusion, anxiety — anything we are going through.

His calls are constant, and He's patient with us as we learn to recognize His voice.

As you read this book, I ask you to be open. Not because you have to—but because He loves you. And here's the truth: **You're holding this book because GOD is trying to talk to you.**

Not just for you to recognize His name on your caller ID— But for you to save His number and start the most incredible relationship of your life, whenever you are ready to do so.

He's not forcing you. He's simply calling.

And the beautiful thing is—He's patient, He's kind, and He'll wait.
Because His love for you has no deadline.

It's eternal.

But the question still remains...

Will you answer?

Chapter 2

Why Is He Really Calling You?

Again, because He loves you in a way no human being can ... in ways you cannot imagine and have not experienced to date.

"For I am persuaded that neither death nor life, nor angels nor principalities nor powers, nor things present nor things to come, nor height nor depth, nor any other created thing, shall be able to separate us from the love of God which is in Christ Jesus our Lord."
— Romans 8:38–39 (NKJV)

This verse beautifully reassures us that nothing can separate us from GOD's love—no mistake, no failure, no struggle. He keeps calling us, waiting for us, pursuing us relentlessly, because His love is unwavering and unconditional.

But there is one thing that can prevent us from fully experiencing His love—**ourselves**.

If we continue to ignore His calls, we close ourselves off from the depth of that love, even though it is always available to us.

Before I started answering His calls, I read about His love. I heard about it. But honestly? I couldn't understand it. How could I grasp something I couldn't physically see or hold in my hands?

So, I ignored Him.

It was easier to rely on what I could see and feel—the things of the physical world, the fleeting highs of life. Work. Money. People. Status. Recognition. Popularity. Things. Temporary pleasures.

At least those gave me what I thought I needed in the moment.

Think about it—don't you remember the **first car** you desperately wanted? The **first job** you craved? The **first relationship** you pursued?

Didn't they bring you instant gratification?

So why bother with GOD—something so abstract, something so complex—when I could chase what felt real and immediate?

Why would I rely on GOD's calls, when I could rely on myself?

Even if He existed, He could wait.
I was chasing other things—things I assumed I needed.
Things that gave me what I wanted and needed, or so I thought.

But then, something shifted. I started to see it—GOD wasn't calling to take away the things I thought I needed and wanted. In fact, sometimes He was removing them because He had something greater planned for me.
He didn't force me to answer. But His calls continued—persistent, gentle, always present, waiting for me to realize that His love was so much greater than anything I was chasing.

Have you ever gone through something in life and later said something like this?
"Oh, I shouldn't have done that!"
"Now I understand why that didn't work."
"I get why that happened."
"I wish I had waited."

That's why GOD is constantly calling us with that persistent and subtle voice ringing in our hearts...

To lead us to something greater.

To direct our steps—especially when our desires start pulling us in the wrong direction.

To protect us from something that will hurt us.

To love us.

"As the heavens are higher than the earth, so are My ways higher than your ways and My thoughts than your thoughts." — Isaiah 55:8–9 (NIV)

Why does He keep reaching out —despite how often we ignore Him?

Because He's not just any god.
He's the Creator of this universe.
Our Creator.

Our Holy Father.

As our Father, He cares for us. He wants to protect us, guide us, and help us thrive.

He wants you to know that He is calling you because **He sees what you cannot.**
He knows the desires, struggles, and pains you are carrying right now.
He loves you so much that He wants you to trust Him with whatever you are going through.
He knows the end from the beginning—and He knows exactly what you need so you can fully enjoy what He has in store for you.

"For I know the plans I have for you, declares the Lord, plans to prosper you and not to harm you, plans to give you hope and a future." — Jeremiah 29:11 (NIV)

His calls aren't pushy or persistent like a spammer.

He simply waits.

He doesn't leave you a voicemail every time He calls. He doesn't send you a dozen follow-up messages. He just wants you to know He is there for you.

He wants you to know that He is there....

When you are seeking something new: a new experience, a new desire.

When you are struggling.

When you feel lost.

When you need help.

"So do not fear, for I am with you; do not be dismayed, for I am your God.
I will strengthen you and help you; I will uphold you with My righteous right hand." —Isaiah 41:10 (NIV)

This verse beautifully captures GOD's presence in our searching, struggles, confusion, and need for help— assuring us that He is there through it all.

That's why He is calling you...
Because He loves you in ways you cannot imagine.

It's something indescribable.
It's something unexplainable.
But it's something so fulfilling and peaceful that you will long for His calls forever more.

Are you ready to experience a love that knows no limits?

Are you ready to be fully seen and fully loved by the One who knows you better than you know yourself?

I invite you to pause for a moment and reflect on how GOD has called you all these years.

Close your eyes, take a deep breath, and allow Him to speak to you.

His love is real, and He's waiting for you to open your heart.

You don't have to understand it all—just be willing to receive the love that's been chasing you.

Chapter 3

The Call That Changed Everything

I was in my late twenties when I finally answered GOD's first call.

Up until then, I had ignored every call He made. I was too busy chasing money, building my career, and planning the life I had envisioned since my teenage years.

I didn't want anything to distract me from **my plan.**

But GOD knew where I was headed—a life filled with disappointment, misery, and despair. That's why He kept calling. **He loved me too much to give up on me, no matter how many times I rejected Him.**

"The Lord Himself goes before you and will be with you; He will never leave you nor forsake you. Do not be afraid; do not be discouraged." — Deuteronomy 31:8 (NIV)

Then, a call I didn't expect came in.

In 2013, I was married, and we had decided it was time to have a child.

Little did I know what GOD had planned for me.

During a routine pregnancy checkup, the doctor mentioned there was a possibility our son could have Down syndrome. I still remember the moment we walked out of that appointment, holding onto a statistic—a 1 in 1,000 chance. **A 0.1% possibility.** It felt so small, so unlikely...

But deep inside, I already knew. **It wasn't a 0.1% chance—it was 100%.**

I was shocked. No one in my family had Down syndrome, and my misconceptions about it made negative thoughts flood my mind. But strangely, even as a non-believer at the time, I knew GOD was behind this.

How did I know?

When I asked the doctor why this happened, he simply said: "This is a random event."

That's when something clicked inside me: *Nothing in this world is random.*

In that moment, something deeper stirred. A quiet awareness that something beyond this world—maybe even GOD Himself—was moving in my life.

That this wasn't chance.

This was intentional.

This was personal.

We went ahead with further testing. This time, the results came back showing a 1 in 4 chance that my son, Lucas, had Down syndrome. When I saw the report, it didn't surprise me. Again, I already knew. But I didn't understand why.

Why would GOD do something like this?

My ego saw it as punishment for ignoring His calls.

But in reality, GOD was saving me—through my son.

He was pulling me away from idolatry, love of money, the lust of life, and the things of this world.

In Canada, abortion is an option. And I contemplated it.

That's when GOD called me—through my wife.

She looked at me and said: "Jose, if GOD gave us a child with Down syndrome, it's because we can bear it. He will give us the strength to do this."

"I can do all things through Christ who strengthens me."
— Philippians 4:13 (NKJV)

At that moment, I hadn't told her I was considering abortion. But GOD knew.

So, He called me—through her—to show me that my desire to end this pregnancy wasn't aligned with His plan for me. It was rooted in fear and uncertainty.

And through her, He told me simply:
"Trust Me—and trust her."

"For God has not given us a spirit of fear, but of power and of love and of a sound mind."
— 2 Timothy 1:7 (NKJV)

I chose to trust her, but still, I did not acknowledge Him as the ONE behind everything.

In hindsight…

Little did I know why He called her and not me.
And little did I know why He asked me to trust her.
Because it was her He was going to give the
supernatural strength to bear this battle.
He knew I was too weak and too selfish at that point in
my life.
He had different plans for each of us.

Six months after Lucas was born, I left our marriage…

Not because of Lucas, but because…

I was overwhelmed—lost in my emotions and life.

I was chasing money and career success—the things the
world teaches us to love.

I was far too focused on building my company, free from
distractions.

I make no excuses for my choice. It's not what I would do
today.

Still, I believe GOD saw all of it.

He knew my heart—even in its weakness.

And He cared.

He cared for me.

He cared for her.

And He cared deeply for our son.

From the moment I walked away from our marriage, she was filled…

with a supernatural strength to care for Lucas.

Strength that only GOD can provide.

"He gives power to the weak, and to those who have no might He increases strength. Even the youths shall faint and be weary, and the young men shall utterly fall, but those who wait on the Lord shall renew their strength; they shall mount up with wings like eagles, they shall run and not be weary, they shall walk and not faint." —Isaiah 40:29–31 (NKJV)

"The Lord is close to the brokenhearted and saves those who are crushed in spirit." —Psalm 34:18 (NIV)

Although I went back to chasing money, growing my career, and building the life I had dreamed of in my teens, **GOD's call—and my son—had already changed me**, even though I didn't know it was Him.

He had planted a seed in me. I had His number now.

Before, I was chasing money.
Now, I was chasing purpose.
Instead of building a career for selfish financial gain,
I poured myself into creating inclusive businesses—a
mission-driven career where I could hire people with
disabilities and raise awareness for their communities.

Because of one call, my entire purpose in life shifted.

Sometimes, GOD calls not just to guide us through our
struggles—but to protect us from making decisions that
will haunt us for the rest of our lives.

If we had gone through with that abortion …
If I had ignored His call at that moment …

I would have destroyed my soul.

To this day, I thank GOD for saving me.
Lucas is not just a blessing. He saved my life.

Not in the dramatic, movie-scene kind of way.

But in the way that only a child with a disability can.

In the way his presence softened my pride.

In the way his vulnerability exposed my own.

In the way loving him forced me to confront the broken parts of myself I had ignored for years.

He saved my life by interrupting my selfishness.

By shifting my priorities.

By reminding me what matters most.

Lucas was the beginning of a new chapter—not just as a father, but as a man waking up to the reality that GOD was calling me all along.

That first call—though I didn't stay on the line for long—was the beginning of a change I never could have imagined.

I am also deeply grateful for my ex-wife.
Because through her, I saw the strength that only GOD can provide.

Looking back, I know I failed her.
Not because I didn't care, but because I didn't have the courage, maturity, or clarity to step up when it mattered most.

I can't undo the choices I made.
And I won't pretend they didn't leave a mark.
But what I've learned is this: even in my weakness—even in my failure—GOD was still present.

He was faithful to her.
Faithful to me.
Faithful to Lucas.
And somehow, He's been redeeming the story ever since.

"But you, Lord, are a compassionate and gracious God, slow to anger, abounding in love and faithfulness."
— Psalm 86:15 (NIV)

Though we are now separated, my ex-wife and I have a healthy, respectful relationship, and I thank GOD for that.

And my relationship with Lucas is being healed, restored, and reshaped by GOD, day by day.

There's still work to do, but I see His hand in every breakthrough, every shared smile, every moment of connection that once felt impossible.

And I'm learning that fatherhood, like faith, is a journey of grace—not perfection.

So, are you ready to pick up His next call?

Even if it's just for a moment, He promises it will change your life in ways you cannot imagine.

I dare you to answer—even if you feel like hanging up after He speaks to you!

Chapter 4

He's Calling You into Relationship, Not Religion

When I finally started answering His calls, I expected rules and restrictions. I thought He wanted to change everything about my life, to convert me into a religion, and to place constraints on me.

But I was wrong.

He wasn't calling me to religion. He was calling me to a relationship.

We are His children—His sons, His daughters.

He created us not to abandon us, but to be present when we need Him most.

This world can be overwhelming, unstable, and cruel— sometimes more often than not. But GOD promises that no matter what we face, He will never leave us:

"He will never leave you nor forsake you."
— Deuteronomy 31:6 (NIV)

GOD's presence is constant. He doesn't turn away from those who seek Him.

He was calling to guide me in my confusion.
He was calling to help me in my despair.
He was calling to show me how much He loved me.
He was calling to be there as my Holy Father.
He was calling me to lead others back to Him.

Again, I ignored His calls because I thought He was seeking to take something away from me—my freedom, my identity, my way of life. I thought He was calling me to religious rules, to a structure I didn't want.

But little did I know...

His "religion" is called love.

And He proved it when He sacrificed His only Son, Jesus Christ, for us.

GOD's love has nothing to do with control or restriction, as I once believed. The way the world portrays religion had distorted my view of Him. But GOD is not a religion—He is a relationship.

A relationship built on:

· **Grace, mercy, and forgiveness** — on His part.
· **Faith, trust, and love** —on our part.

He doesn't call us to rules. He calls us to Him.
And once we step into that relationship, everything begins to change—not because of obligation, but because of love.

And just like any true relationship, love takes time and effort to cultivate. But unlike human relationships, **GOD never changes—we are the ones who change.**

We are the ones who pull away, who ignore His calls, who distance ourselves when we don't understand His ways.

Imagine calling someone repeatedly, knowing they were intentionally ignoring you.

Would you keep calling? Would you still want to help them?

Most of us would eventually give up. We might even delete their number or block them altogether.

But that's how I know **His love for us is different.**

His love is unwavering.

It does not fluctuate with emotions or circumstances.

It is not fragile or conditional.

His love is steadfast.

"The steadfast love of the Lord never ceases; His mercies never come to an end; they are new every morning; great is your faithfulness." — Lamentations 3:22–23 (ESV)

His love is full of promises—promises written in His word, promises He will never break.

Because **GOD's nature is unchanging, faithful, and true.**

Unlike people, He does not lie or fail to fulfill what He has spoken.

- **GOD's character is faithful** — *"God is not human, that He should lie, not a human being, that He should change His mind. Does He speak and then not act? Does He promise and not fulfill?"* — *Numbers 23:19 (NIV)*

- **His Word is eternal** —*"The grass withers, the flower fades, but the word of our God will stand forever."* — *Isaiah 40:8 (ESV)*

- **He is bound by His own nature** — *"If we are faithless, He remains faithful, for He cannot deny Himself."* — *2 Timothy 2:13 (ESV)*

- **His promises are fulfilled in Christ** — *"For no matter how many promises God has made, they are 'Yes' in Christ.* — *2 Corinthians 1:20 (NIV)*

GOD's love doesn't fade, doesn't fail, and doesn't forget.
Even when we ignore Him, He still calls.
Even when we run, He still pursues.

Because to Him, **we were never just another number in His phonebook—He wrote our names on His hands.**

"See, I have written your name on the palms of My hands. — *Isaiah 49:16 (NLT)*

The same hands used to create this infinite and amazing universe.
The same hands pierced for our sins, in Jesus Christ—our Savior, our Redeemer, our only way back to the Father.

So next time He calls, remember—He's not reaching out to talk about religion. He's calling because He knows you need Him. Whether it's guidance, direction, answers, companionship, or validation—whatever it is, He's reaching out with love, ready to give you what only He can.

"Your word is a lamp to my feet and a light to my path."
— Psalm 119:105 (NIV)

He has everything you need for whatever you are going through, whether that's clarity, wisdom, love, peace, or joy. He knows exactly what you need. Just ask Him.

"If any of you lacks wisdom, you should ask God, who gives generously to all without finding fault, and it will be given to you." — James 1:5 (NIV)

Remember, He is your Creator and Holy Father.
He knows why He created you.

"Before I formed you in the womb I knew you, before you were born I set you apart; I appointed you as a prophet to the nations." — Jeremiah 1:5 (NIV)

GOD's intentions for us are always good and always filled with hope and purpose.

GOD isn't calling you to follow rules.
He's calling you to follow Him.
Because what He wants isn't your performance.
He wants your heart.

Chapter 5

How Does GOD Get Your Phone Number?

Let me start by saying this: He doesn't need to get your number from anyone because...

He is the **Creator of the Universe.**

"In the beginning, God created the heavens and the earth." — *Genesis 1:1 (ESV)*

"For this is what the Lord says—He who created the heavens, He is God; He who fashioned and made the earth, He founded it; He did not create it to be empty, but formed it to be inhabited—He says: 'I am the Lord, and there is no other.'" — *Isaiah 45:18 (NIV)*

These verses remind us that GOD, as the Creator, designed the universe with intention and purpose. Nothing exists outside His knowledge—**including us.**

Our creator knows us completely.

"Then God said, 'Let Us make mankind in Our image, in Our likeness, so that they may rule over the fish in the sea and the birds in the sky, over the livestock and all the wild animals, and over all the creatures that move along the ground.' So God created mankind in His own image, in the image of God He created them; male and female He created them." — Genesis 1:26–27 (NIV)

We are not just random beings—GOD made us in His image. He knows everything about us, including our deepest thoughts and desires. If an artist knows their masterpiece and a car manufacturer knows every cylinder in an engine, **how much more does our Creator know us?**

He is a loving Father, not a controlling master.

"The Spirit you received does not make you slaves, so that you live in fear again; rather, the Spirit you received brought about your adoption to sonship. And by Him we cry, 'Abba, Father.'" — Romans 8:15 (NIV)

GOD doesn't just know you—**He is your Abba Father.** The term "Abba" signifies an intimate, loving relationship. Unlike an overbearing authority, He gives us free will, trusting that in time, we will seek His guidance.

"Because you are His sons, God sent the Spirit of His Son into our hearts, the Spirit who calls out, 'Abba, Father.' So you are no longer a slave, but God's child; and since you are His child, God has made you also an heir." — *Galatians 4:6–7 (NIV)*

GOD invites, but He never forces.

He respects our choices, even when we ignore Him.

He is not a possessive Father who wants to control our lives, restraining us from things or even controlling our decisions.

Instead, He gives you the freedom to choose, trusting that in your heart, you will seek His guidance. His love is one that respects your will and is always there to support and guide you when you turn to Him.

But when someone gives GOD your number ...

His calls may become more obvious and persistent in your life.

Why? Because someone who loves you has been praying for you.

Love moves this world, and it originates in GOD. People who have experienced His love want to share it. They see your struggles, your burdens, and your unanswered questions, and they intercede on your behalf.

"I urge, then, first of all, that petitions, prayers, intercession, and thanksgiving be made for all people— for kings and all those in authority, that we may live peaceful and quiet lives in all godliness and holiness."
— 1 Timothy 2:1–2 (NIV)

Intercession is an act of love. It could come from your mother or father, a family member, a friend, your spouse, or even a stranger.

Why would they do that?

Because they know you need help with something you are going through or a decision you need to make. They care for you, they love you, and they know you need help, support, and guidance even though you think you don't need it. They love so much that they are willing to intercede for you.

That's the beauty of GOD's love.

It reaches you in unexpected ways

It's accessible to anyone and for everyone.

"For God so loved the world that He gave His one and only Son, that whoever believes in Him shall not perish but have eternal life." — John 3:16 (NIV)

What does this mean for you?

When you feel GOD's calls more strongly—when His presence tugs at your heart—remember this: Someone cared enough to pray for you. Someone invested their time, energy, and faith so that you might encounter GOD in a new way.

Would you ignore a heartfelt gift given to you at Christmas?

Would you dismiss a letter written with love?

Now that you know this, will you answer His next call?

Because when someone gives GOD your number…
He never forgets it.

Chapter 6

My Mom Gave GOD My Phone Number

Like I said, GOD already has your phone number—He doesn't need anyone to give it to Him.

However, there are people in your life who ask GOD to give you a call. In life, someone might refer you to a person they believe can help you. Intercessory prayer works the same way.

Someone—a relative, a friend, or even a stranger—might feel that you need GOD and that you would benefit from a call from Him. **And GOD, being our loving Father, delights in reaching out to His children.**

Because He loves you in a way no human being ever could… in ways beyond your imagination.

So when someone close to Him says, "Lord, give Your child a call; they need You," His heart overflows with joy.

How does this happen?

Simple. Through intercessory prayer.

"I looked for someone among them who would build up the wall and stand before me in the gap on behalf of the land..." — Ezekiel 22:30 (NIV)

Intercessory prayer is powerful because it invites GOD's divine intervention into someone else's life. When we intercede, we stand in the gap, lifting their struggles, desires, and needs before Him. Even if we don't see immediate results, make no mistake—He hears those prayers.

Praying for others can bring healing, strength, and transformation. When offered with faith, our prayers have real impact.

What does intercessory prayer do?

It opens the door for GOD's will.

Even if someone isn't actively seeking GOD, He responds to the faithful prayers of others.

"The effective, fervent prayer of a righteous man avails much." — James 5:16 (NKJV)

It brings spiritual protection and breakthroughs.

We don't just face physical struggles, but spiritual ones as well. Intercession helps break strongholds that keep people from answering GOD's calls.

"For we do not wrestle against flesh and blood, but against principalities, against powers, against the rulers of the darkness of this age, against spiritual hosts of wickedness in the heavenly places."
— Ephesians 6:12 (NKJV)

It softens hearts toward GOD.

Many reject GOD due to pain, past wounds, or spiritual blindness. Prayer helps remove those barriers.

"I will give you a new heart and put a new spirit within you; I will take the heart of stone out of your flesh and give you a heart of flesh." — Ezekiel 36:26 (NKJV)

It brings healing and restoration.

GOD heals not only physically but emotionally and spiritually through the prayers of others.

"Is anyone among you sick? Let him call for the elders of the church, and let them pray over him, anointing him with oil in the name of the Lord. And the prayer of faith will save the sick, and the Lord will raise him up." — *James 5:14–15 (NKJV)*

It releases GOD's peace and strength.

Even when someone isn't aware they are being prayed for, intercession can bring supernatural peace.

"And the peace of God, which surpasses all understanding, will guard your hearts and minds through Christ Jesus." — *Philippians 4:7 (NKJV)*

That's what my mother did for me—she interceded for me...

Although I had answered one of GOD's calls when my son was diagnosed with Down syndrome, I continued to ignore His calls afterward. My mother saw the fruit of my life and knew I was drifting away from GOD.

She saw it in the way I lived:

Lust and temptation through my romantic relationships.

Self-reliance through my professional career and business pursuits.

Fear and anxiety that followed me in everything I did.

Division and strife that plagued my relationships with family and friends.

She knew I was seeking something beyond myself but I was resisting seeking GOD wholeheartedly.

Instead of acknowledging Him, I idolized His creation—calling Him "the Universe" instead of "GOD."

I placed my trust in money, relationships, and even new age practices—yoga, meditation, Buddhism, spiritual rituals, and crystals—rather than in the Creator Himself.

She tried to reason with me, but the more she spoke, the more I pulled away—not only from GOD but from her. **So, she turned to a different realm: the spiritual one.** She fought for me through intercessory prayer…

And GOD answered.

I recall many moments when I felt His grace and mercy reaching for me through life's trials.

My mother's prayers weakened the enemy's grip and allowed GOD's power to move.

You may wonder…

Why does GOD need intercessory prayer if He can do anything?

He doesn't need it—but He chooses to use it, inviting us to be part of His divine work.

He could act without our prayers, but He desires relationship, not control.

Intercessory prayer isn't about changing GOD's mind—it's about aligning with His will and inviting heaven's power to earth.

"This is the confidence we have in approaching God: that if we ask anything according to His will, He hears us. And if we know that He hears us—whatever we ask—we know that we have what we asked of Him."
— 1 John 5:14–15 (NIV)

For those of us who are far from GOD, it's easy to underestimate the spiritual battle at play. Many of our struggles aren't just physical; they are rooted in the unseen realm.

That's why intercessory prayer is critical.

It blocks distractions the enemy places in our path, clearing the way for us to hear GOD's calls.

It silences unhealthy voices so we can answer the right one.

So, who is interceding for you?

I can tell you this—**someone is.**

How do I know? Because you are loved more than you realize.

"Christ Jesus who died—more than that, who was raised to life—is at the right hand of GOD and is also interceding for us." — Romans 8:34 (NIV)

Jesus Himself is praying for you.

And I believe someone else is too—just like my mother prayed for me. Maybe it's your mother, father, sibling, friend, or even a stranger. But if you still think no one else is interceding for you, let me tell you this:

I am.

That's why I wrote this book.

Know this: **you are not forgotten**.

And as you keep reading, I pray this truth settles in your heart:
You're not alone, and you never were.
GOD's been calling you all along—
Not to burden you, but to bring you back to Him.

So pick up. Your life is about to change!

Chapter 7

The Distraction That Made Me Miss His Calls

I ghosted GOD for almost ten years before I realized how much I needed Him.

He kept calling me, especially after my child, Lucas, was born. But I made it clear—I wanted nothing to do with GOD. I was too focused on the things of this world.

How do I know that now?

Because my actions reflected the condition of my heart.

Blind ambition. Selfishness. Pride. Hardened conscience.

I was chasing money, recognition, popularity, and career success—the things the world teaches us to love. And in pursuit of those things, I did the unthinkable…

I left my child—my own flesh and blood, born with Down syndrome—just six months after he entered this world. I abandoned my wife at the time, leaving her to care for our son alone. And for what? To build my company, free from distractions so I could accomplish those things.

At least, that's what I told myself.

The truth? My heart had already been drawn elsewhere. I had started developing feelings for a coworker, and instead of resisting it, I followed where my heart led me.

I made my heart my biggest distraction.

"The heart is deceitful above all things and desperately wicked: who can know it?" — Jeremiah 17:9 (KJV)

My heart, unchecked and unsubmitted to GOD, became an instrument for the enemy. Satan thrives on deception, and he whispers just enough truth to make lies feel right. When our hearts are not anchored in GOD, they become easy prey.

"But Peter said, 'Ananias, why has Satan filled your heart to lie to the Holy Spirit...?" — Acts 5:3 (NKJV)

Satan had filled my heart with lies. And I believed them.

Culture says, "Follow your heart"...

That was the lie that led me away from GOD—straight into destruction.

Though I never acted on my adulterous feelings, the enemy had already succeeded. He had created division between me and the people I loved. And ultimately, he had created division between me and GOD.

I abandoned my family. I threw myself into work, believing success would validate me instead.

But it didn't stop there. My hunger for more only grew:

- **More growth.**
- **More recognition.**
- **More validation.**
- **More of everything.**

And the enemy fueled that hunger with his lies:

- *"You are not enough."*

- *"They are better than you."*

- *"You have to prove your worth."*

- *"If you work harder, then you'll be valuable."*

- *"Once you hit your next goal, then you'll be fulfilled."*

I believed every single lie. And I acted on them.

Even after my child was born, when I had shifted from chasing just money to building impactful companies, I was still pursuing worldly things.

I lied to get what I wanted. I manipulated people to advance my company. I idolized men like Steve Jobs and Elon Musk, measuring my worth by their standards. I disrespected my parents because they didn't align with my ambitions. I was never content, always envying what others had.

"But each person is tempted when he is lured and enticed by his own desire. Then desire, when it has conceived, gives birth to sin, and sin, when it is fully grown, brings forth death." — James 1:14–15 (ESV)

The enemy had already destroyed my marriage and convinced me to walk away from my home just months after Lucas was born. Then he went after the company I had sacrificed everything to build—using my own ambition to twist my priorities. But Satan wasn't finished. His goal wasn't just to ruin my life. His aim was far more dangerous: to harden my heart, turn me against GOD, and lure me into embracing his counterfeit version of life.

Why would Satan want to keep you from GOD?

Because he knows what he lost.

Satan wasn't always the enemy. He was once a glorious angel, created by GOD.

But pride corrupted him.

Instead of worshiping his Creator, he wanted to be equal to Him.

He rebelled—and was cast out of heaven.

"You were the signet of perfection, full of wisdom and perfect in beauty… You were blameless in your ways from the day you were created, till unrighteousness was found in you… Your heart was proud because of your beauty; you corrupted your wisdom for the sake of your splendor." — Ezekiel 28:12–17 (ESV)

His fate was sealed. And now, his mission is to ensure as many of us as possible share in his downfall.

How does he do that?

By keeping us distracted with his worldly things.

By getting us to believe and act on his lies.

By convincing us that sin is satisfying.

By keeping us so busy chasing temporary things that we never stop to answer GOD's calls.

Because once we truly turn to GOD, we step into the love, purpose, and redemption that Satan can never have again.

And that terrifies him.

But here's the good news: No matter how long we've ignored Him, GOD never stops calling.
His love is relentless. His mercy is unending. And He is always ready to take us back.

But we must choose to return. And that choice begins with repentance.

REPENTANCE is our way of calling back to GOD, saying, "I need You."

During those years, He never stopped calling me. He never stopped working through circumstances and people to remind me that He was there.

But I hadn't realized that yet.

And Satan knew it. He'd already torn apart my marriage, strained my relationship with my child, and twisted my priorities.

But he wasn't done. Now, he targeted a deeper longing—the one thing I was craving most in that season: **love.**

He wanted to keep destroying me quietly, in a way that didn't look like destruction.

After years of being single, I finally decided to put myself out there again. I was searching for love and companionship, for someone who would make me feel joyful. And I found someone.

At the time, I was not aware GOD had placed that person in my life as a blessing. But now looking back, I see that He placed her there not just as a blessing but also as a lesson—to show me just how lost I was, how entangled I had become in the enemy's deception.

She was a divine message sent by GOD.

He uses people to reveal what we're blind to in ourselves.

How do I know?

Again, because that experience revealed the true condition of my heart.

Insecurity. Selfishness. Pride. Deception.

I lied. I cheated. I mistreated her.

I had not only deceived others—I had deceived myself.

I convinced myself that my actions were justified, that I wasn't really hurting anyone, that I could keep control of the situation. But deception always has a price. I ignored my conscience, silenced the truth, and let my desires lead me.

And when it all fell apart, I saw the full extent of the damage I had done.

Not only had I hurt myself, I had hurt someone I deeply cared for.

And worst of all, I had hurt GOD.

I remember coming back to our apartment after she had moved out, after she had discovered my betrayal. The silence in that space was deafening. It wasn't just the absence of her—it was the weight of GOD's judgment pressing down on me.

For the first time, I truly saw myself.

GOD showed me who I had become.

I had become a wicked and evil man—far from who GOD had created me to be.

That day, I made a vow to myself: I would never live like that again.

I repented.

I felt genuine remorse. I knew no one deserved the pain I had caused. Especially not someone I had claimed to love.

I wanted nothing to do with that life anymore.

Looking back, I now see that in that moment—without even realizing it—I had taken my first step back toward GOD.

And He heard me.

He knew I was finally ready for Him.

The only question was...

How long was it going to take me to finally acknowledge and accept Him—
As my Creator?
As my Holy Father?

I had missed so many of His calls.
But that day, I finally picked up.
And the voice on the other end wasn't angry.
It was love.
Pure, undeserved, redemptive love.

The kind only a Heavenly Father can give.

Chapter 8

Why People Ignore GOD's Call (and How to Stop)

Although we may think we're the ones ignoring GOD's calls, the truth is that the world and its culture influence us—both consciously and unconsciously—to do so.

Satan, as the ruler of this world, has masterfully crafted distractions that pull us away from GOD, but his reign is temporary. Christ has already overcome him.

"Now is the judgment of this world; now will the ruler of this world be cast out." — John 12:31 (ESV)

Until we recognize this, we will struggle to break free. **This world offers only temporary pleasures**, and no matter what we achieve, our lives will feel empty and unfulfilled.

The enemy's tactics are deliberate and often subtle. He will keep us separated from GOD, bound by distractions, as long as we let him.

Don't let him.

GOD's way is infinitely better—there is no comparison!

When you answer His calls, He will reveal Himself to you.

"As for God, His way is perfect: The Lord's word is flawless; He shields all who take refuge in Him."
— Psalm 18:30 (NIV)

These are some of the ways the world distracts and deceives us:

1. *"Follow your heart"*

The world tells us to "follow our hearts," but Scripture warns that the heart is deceitful (Jeremiah 17:9). When we trust our emotions over GOD's truth, we set ourselves up for disappointment, pain, and misguided decisions. Feelings change—GOD's Word does not.

2. *"Live for yourself"*

Selfish ambition, pride, and self-centeredness pull us away from GOD's purpose. The world glorifies these things, but they lead to confusion and disorder (James 3:14–16). And in the process, we often hurt the very people we love most. True fulfillment comes not from serving ourselves but from living for GOD and serving others—only then can we find lasting peace.

3. *"Chase money, success, and power"*

The world says that wealth, status, and influence will bring happiness, but Jesus tells us that we cannot serve both GOD and money (Matthew 6:24). No matter how much success we achieve, it will never be enough to fill the void in our hearts. In the end, chasing these things will only leave us drained, empty, and searching for more.

4. *"Seek pleasure above all else"*

Lust, addiction, and entertainment keep us distracted from our spiritual hunger (Galatians 5:19–21). The world promotes indulgence, making it seem like the key to happiness, but it only leaves us emptier. Things like FOMO (Fear of Missing Out) and YOLO (You Only Live Once) feed an addiction to adrenaline and constant novelty—keeping us restless, unfulfilled, and spiritually disconnected. These distractions only deepen the hunger in our souls.

5. *"Love yourself" and "Be yourself"*

The enemy wants us to believe we are unworthy, unloved, or too far gone for grace (John 8:44). At the same time, the world tells us that self-love and self-reliance are the keys to happiness. But when we make ourselves the center, we become blind to the needs of others. True identity isn't found in "being yourself" but in being who GOD created you to be. Christ didn't come to help us "be ourselves"—He came to make us new in Him.

6. *"Stay busy and distracted"*

Overworking, endless entertainment, and mindless scrolling drown out GOD's voice (Luke 10:41–42). One of the enemy's greatest weapons is busyness—keeping us so occupied with the external world that we don't have the time or space to connect with GOD. But when we finally slow down, we feel lost and empty because our souls were created to be with Him. In this chaos, we miss the stillness where GOD speaks the loudest.

7. *"Doubt GOD's Word and promises"*

From the very beginning, the enemy's strategy has been to make us question what GOD has said (Genesis 3:1–5). Today, talking about GOD, His Word, and His promises is often met with skepticism—even among believers. The world has taught people to doubt GOD at every level, including His role in creation (Genesis 1:1–31). But truth remains truth, no matter how much the world denies it. We must fight the enemy's lies with the unshakable foundation of GOD's Word.

8. *"Create your own truth"*

The world tells us that truth is subjective—that what's "right" for one person may not be right for another, varying across ethnic, cultural, religious, and geographical contexts. But GOD's truth never changes (Isaiah 5:20). When we compromise on what He has declared right and wrong, we begin shaping truth to fit our desires instead of allowing truth to shape us. In reality, truth is not up for negotiation—it's divinely established.

9. *"You are in control"*

The world conditions us to rely on our own strength, making us believe that if we don't have full control, things will fall apart. This leads to anxiety and fear. But GOD never intended for us to carry that weight alone. He calls us to trust Him completely, knowing that He is in control and has already secured our future (2 Timothy 1:7). When we surrender our fears to Him, He replaces them with His perfect peace. The burden of control isn't ours to bear—it's His.

10. "GOD is not real"

The world wants you to believe that you're better off alone and without GOD—that no one understands you, that GOD is distant, or that people will judge you if you believe in Him. But spiritual isolation is a trap. When we withdraw from GOD and community, we become easy targets for doubt, discouragement, and deception. GOD created us for relationship—with Him and with others (Hebrews 10:25). The enemy's greatest weapon is isolation. Don't fall for it.

Consider some of the world's most successful marketing campaigns:

"A Diamond Is Forever" — *De Beers*

"Open Happiness" — *Coca-Cola*

"What Happens Here, Stays Here" — *Las Vegas Tourism*

"It Gives You Wings" — *Red Bull*

"It Keeps Going and Going and Going" — *Energizer*

Similarly, the enemy runs his own deceptive campaigns. But his goal isn't to inspire or empower you—it's to separate you from GOD.

His messages are carefully crafted to keep you bound, enslaved to fleeting pleasures. He convinces you that sin satisfies, that distractions fulfill, and that you don't need GOD.

And the world plays along, keeping you enslaved to the noise. The more you indulge in its distractions, the more distant GOD seems—even though He's never stopped calling.

But here's the good news...

Jesus has already defeated the world.

How did He do it?

By living a life free from distractions, fully connected to GOD in everything He did.

By answering all of GOD's calls.

By dying and rising again—conquering sin, death, and the enemy.

"In this world you will have trouble. But take heart! I have overcome the world." — John 16:33 (NIV)

Through Jesus, we are set free from these traps.

That's why He's calling.

He wants to guide us, just as the Father guided Him.

"So if the Son sets you free, you will be free indeed." — *John 8:36 (NIV)*

I'm not saying you need to be Jesus—there is only one begotten Son—but through Him, we find the strength to overcome these distractions and reconnect with our Creator, our Holy Father.

"I can do all things through Christ who strengthens me." — *Philippians 4:13 (NKJV)*

Now that you recognize what's been distracting you—and the One who can help you overcome those distractions—let's talk about how to break free and start answering GOD's calls.

1. Follow GOD's Word *(instead of following your heart)*

Instead of following your heart, follow His Word. Your emotions will change, but GOD's truth remains the same. Make Scripture the foundation of your decisions, not fleeting feelings.

"Your word is a lamp to my feet and a light to my path." — *Psalm 119:105 (ESV)*

2. Live for GOD *(instead of living for yourself)*

The world tells you to live for yourself, but real purpose is found in living for Him. When you surrender your desires to GOD, He replaces them with something far greater— His perfect will.

"Whoever wants to be My disciple must deny themselves and take up their cross daily and follow Me." — *Luke 9:23 (NIV)*

3. Chase GOD, Jesus, and the Holy Spirit *(instead of chasing money, success, and power)*

Instead of chasing money, success, and power, chase after the things of GOD. When you seek Him first, He takes care of the rest.

"But seek first His kingdom and His righteousness, and all these things will be given to you as well." — *Matthew 6:33 (NIV)*

4. Seek righteousness *(instead of seeking pleasure above all else)*

The world promotes pleasure and indulgence, but true fulfillment comes from walking in righteousness. Holiness isn't about rules—it's about staying close to GOD and living in His freedom.

"Blessed are those who hunger and thirst for righteousness, for they will be filled." — Matthew 5:6 (NIV)

5. Be consumed by His love *(instead of loving yourself and being yourself)*

The enemy tries to convince you that you're unworthy, but GOD calls you chosen, loved, and redeemed.

"And so we know and rely on the love God has for us. God is love. Whoever lives in love lives in God, and God in them." — 1 John 4:16 (NIV)

6. Be present with GOD *(instead of staying busy and distracted)*

Distractions can keep you from hearing GOD's voice. Slow down, make space for Him, and be still in His presence.

"Be still, and know that I am God." — Psalm 46:10 (NKJV)

7. Believe His Word and promises *(instead of questioning them)*

The world will tempt you to doubt GOD's Word. But His promises are unshakable. Even when circumstances seem uncertain, stand firm in the truth that He never fails. His Word does not return void, and what He has spoken, He will fulfill.

"Let us hold unswervingly to the hope we profess, for He who promised is faithful." — Hebrews 10:23 (NIV)

8. Stand firm in GOD's truth *(instead of defining your own)*

The world pressures us to accept its version of success and truth, shaping our beliefs to fit its agenda. But GOD calls us to stand firm in *His* truth, even when it's unpopular or countercultural.

"Woe to those who call evil good and good evil, who put darkness for light and light for darkness." — Isaiah 5:20 (NIV)

9. Trust Him with all your heart *(instead of believing you're in control)*

Fear, worry, and the need for control are distractions the enemy uses to keep us from fully surrendering to GOD. But true peace comes when we trust in His sovereignty, knowing that His plans are greater than our own. Letting go isn't weakness—it's faith in action.

"Trust in the Lord with all your heart and lean not on your own understanding; in all your ways submit to Him, and He will make your paths straight."
— *Proverbs 3:5–6 (NIV)*

10. Stay connected to GOD and His people *(instead of cutting yourself off)*

Isolation is one of the enemy's greatest weapons. When we withdraw from GOD and the people He has placed in our lives, we become easy targets for doubt, fear, and deception. But we were never meant to walk this journey alone. GOD calls us to stay rooted in Him and in community, where we can find encouragement, accountability, and strength.

"Not giving up meeting together, as some are in the habit of doing, but encouraging one another—and all the more as you see the Day approaching." — *Hebrews 10:25 (NIV)*

The world will always try to distract you.

The enemy will always try to pull you away from GOD.

But now, you know what's behind the noise—and more importantly, how to rise above it.

You know the lies.

You've seen the traps.

 And now, you've been shown the way out.

GOD is calling.

Will you keep ignoring Him?

Or will you finally stop, pick up, and say, "Yes"?

Will you choose Him today?

Chapter 9

The Stranger GOD Sent to Call Me Back

Although I had accepted the man I had become—a wicked and sinful one—I had also decided to change. I **was ready to repent, to turn away from my wrongdoings.**

The weight of my actions, the pain of my choices, and the judgment I faced felt overwhelming. But in the midst of it all, something stirred within me...

A spiritual hunger unlike anything I had ever known.

For the first time in my life, I wasn't seeking fulfillment from worldly things. I wasn't chasing success, validation, or temporary pleasure.

I was craving peace, longing for something more, desperate for support, yearning for love …

Not romantic love, but something deeper.

I was looking for a spiritual connection that could heal me.

A connection only GOD can provide.

And He was ready to meet me in my need.

He wanted to reveal Himself to me, but He knew I wasn't ready for that just yet.

He knew I wasn't prepared to have a long conversation with Him.

He knew I wasn't ready to acknowledge Him, but He saw that I had begun turning away from the world, and He wanted to help me in a way I could bear.

So instead, He sent someone.

Someone to embody **His love.**
Someone to reflect **His grace.**
Someone to offer me **that connection.**
Someone to make me **a better person.**

Someone to prepare **the way for Him in my life.**

"As iron sharpens iron, so one person sharpens another."
— Proverbs 27:17 (NIV)

How do I know that?

Because that person met me exactly where I was—in my brokenness.

Because that person reflected GOD's character of love, joy, peace, patience, kindness, goodness, faithfulness, gentleness, and self-control.

Because that person made me want to change but did not expect me to change.

Because that person loved me for who I was, who I am, and who I will be, regardless of whether I was with her or not.

She listened, even when my story was harsh and hurt her.

She extended grace, even when I didn't deserve it.

She showed me unconditional love, the kind only GOD can give.

And the most incredible part?

This wasn't a lifelong friend or a family member, or even my partner at the time.

This was a total stranger—someone I had only met a week before.

Yet, through her, GOD was drawing me closer.

"Draw near to God, and He will draw near to you. Cleanse your hands, you sinners, and purify your hearts, you double-minded." — James 4:8 (ESV)

That's how faithful GOD is. That's how much He cares.

I didn't deserve that kind of connection because of what I had just done in my previous relationship.

But again, GOD is gracious and merciful, especially when we repent for our wrongdoings.

He gives us time and opportunities to turn to Him.

GOD longs for all His children to return and rejoice with Him.

"The Lord is not slow in keeping His promise, as some understand slowness. Instead, He is patient with you, not wanting anyone to perish, but everyone to come to repentance." — 2 Peter 3:9 (NIV)

Even though I hadn't acknowledged Him as my Creator, He knew the hunger in my spirit.

He knew I had taken the first step to accepting His calls: **repentance.**

And in response, He sent someone to help guide me toward Him.

Someone who, without even realizing it, aligned me with the Holy Spirit—the very connection I needed to begin hearing GOD's voice when He calls.

Because GOD knew I needed a person who embodied His character, someone who would push me to seek Him.

Someone who would make me think...

What is this? Why does this feel so different?

At first, it was my son, Lucas.

Then, it was the ending of my previous relationship, as I explained in the previous chapter.

And now was the beginning of another relationship with the stranger I introduced in this chapter.

GOD moves in ways we cannot comprehend.

GOD works differently depending on what we are going through.

But make no mistake—**GOD knows you better than you know yourself.**

He works uniquely in all of us—and always in ways we cannot comprehend.

"For My thoughts are not your thoughts, neither are your ways My ways, declares the Lord. For as the heavens are higher than the earth, so are My ways higher than your ways and My thoughts than your thoughts." — Isaiah 55:8–9 (ESV)

And one more thing—GOD does not waste any opportunities to connect with you.

He doesn't waste experiences, lessons, or even our brokenness. He redeems everything for His glory.

GOD loves you so much that even if you don't answer His calls…

He will keep calling you through the very things you desire in life.

Whether that's a relationship, job, career, trip—anything.

He knows that when we are far from Him and haven't accepted Him as our Creator and Holy Father, we are more open to listening to other people and things than we are to Him.

He created all of us to become His message and messenger, even if we don't know it.

He created all of us to conform to His image.

"Then God said, 'Let us make man in Our image, after Our likeness.'" — Genesis 1:26 (ESV)

She, this stranger, was just the beginning—
A glimpse of His grace in the middle of my mess.

Through her, GOD reminded me that He hadn't given up.
That He could still reach me, even when I wasn't reaching for Him.

And GOD?
He was only getting started.

Chapter 10

How GOD Reaches You When You're Not Listening

GOD loves all His children—but His heart burns with urgency for those who are still lost, still wrapped in the enemy's arms. He leaves the ninety-nine to search for the one. He doesn't forget those who are already His, but He will go to any length to chase after the ones who are still lost.

"I have not come to call the righteous, but sinners to repentance." — Luke 5:32 (NIV)

GOD does not want anyone to perish...

"The Lord is not slow in keeping His promise, as some understand slowness. Instead, He is patient with you, not wanting anyone to perish, but everyone to come to repentance." — 2 Peter 3:9 (NIV)

He will use everything at His disposal to get your attention—without violating your free will, especially during that phase when you are ignoring His calls and haven't accepted Him as your Holy Father and His Son as your Lord and Savior.

He respects your freedom and free will.

He will not manipulate you to get your attention.

He knows love is a free choice, and He wants you to reach out to Him...

On your own, from your heart.

However, He is always speaking, always reaching out— you just have to recognize the ways He does it. Here are some powerful ways He can connect with you:

1. Through people

GOD often uses people to guide, encourage, and challenge us. It could be a mentor, a friend, a family member, or even a total stranger who speaks truth and love into your life at the right moment.

"As iron sharpens iron, so one person sharpens another."
— Proverbs 27:17 (NIV)

2. Through life circumstances

GOD can speak through both blessings and hardships. A closed door, a tough season, or an unexpected opportunity may be His way of redirecting you to His purpose.

"And we know that in all things God works for the good of those who love Him, who have been called according to His purpose." — Romans 8:28 (NIV)

3. Through dreams and visions

GOD has used dreams and visions throughout Scripture to communicate with His people, and He still does today. Sometimes, He plants a vision in your heart or speaks to you through dreams to guide you toward His will.

"For God does speak—now one way, now another— though no one perceives it. In a dream, in a vision of the night..." — Job 33:14–15 (NIV)

4. Through nature and creation

GOD's presence can be felt in the beauty around us—the sound of waves, the way flowers bloom, the calm of an early morning. It all points back to Him. Creation reflects His glory and reminds us that He's not just powerful, but intimately near.

"The heavens declare the glory of God; the skies proclaim the work of His hands." — Psalm 19:1 (NIV)

5. Through inner conviction and the Holy Spirit

Sometimes, you just "know" something deep inside—it's that unshakable conviction, a pull in a certain direction, or a peace that surpasses understanding. That's the Holy Spirit leading and guiding you.

"But the Advocate, the Holy Spirit, whom the Father will send in my name, will teach you all things and will remind you of everything I have said to you." — John 14:26 (NIV)

6. Through music

Songs of praise, worship, or even personal moments of singing to GOD can bring His presence closer and speak to your heart in ways words cannot.

"But I will sing of Your strength, in the morning I will sing of Your love; for You are my fortress, my refuge in times of trouble." — Psalm 59:16 (NIV)

7. Through work and calling

Your job, business, or passion can be a place where GOD meets you. He can use your work to shape you, bless others, and draw you closer to Him.

"Whatever you do, work at it with all your heart, as working for the Lord, not for human masters, since you know that you will receive an inheritance from the Lord as a reward. It is the Lord Christ you are serving."
— Colossians 3:23–24 (NIV)

Why would He use these things to connect with us when He can speak directly to you?

Because He does not want to force you to answer His calls or talk to Him.

He wants you to want to talk to Him.

He actually wants you to call Him back.

But He understands you, and He is patient with you.

GOD knows that in the "worldly" phase of our lives…

We are more concerned about the things of this world than the things of Him.

We are not reading His Word and honestly do not believe it.

We haven't accepted Him as our Creator and Holy Father.

We seek spiritual fulfillment in practices like yoga, meditation, crystals, or other new-age beliefs, not realizing that **true fulfillment comes only from a relationship with Him.**

We don't believe in Jesus as His only begotten Son or as our Lord and Savior.

In those moments, our spiritual compass is off. We chase fulfillment elsewhere—trying anything to feel whole, while unknowingly drifting further from the One who can actually restore us.

Praying seems unnatural and pointless.

We love the things of this world—money, recognition, possessions, sex, travel, drugs...

Everything that gives us a quick thrill and helps us avoid stillness with ourselves—and with GOD.

How do I know that? Because that was me back then.

And nothing could convince me otherwise.

When things are going "well" in your life and you keep yourself distracted with these things, it's hard to seek something different. Why would you?

Because...

You feel something deep inside telling you something is off—that spiritual hunger I had.

Because ...

Hardships start happening, and you know the worldly things you tried are not the answer anymore.

Something very deep inside—the Holy Spirit—is telling you it's Him.

He is the answer to everything.

In my case, GOD used people and relationships to lead me back to Him.

He knew that was the only way I would hear Him.

However, this is not the case for everyone.

And He can use a combination of things to grab your attention...

As He's done with me.

The question is not whether GOD is speaking to you—but whether you are ready to recognize His voice and respond.

GOD is always speaking.

Sometimes it's through people.

Other times through pain.

Sometimes in nature.

Other times through restlessness.

And sometimes, through the very silence you try to avoid.

But **He's always calling.**

Even when you ignore Him.

Even when you run.

Even when you think you're too far gone.

He's not waiting to punish you.

He's waiting to love you.

So if you've been wondering why certain people, patterns, or pain keep showing up in your life...

Maybe it's not random.

Maybe it's not coincidence.

Maybe—just maybe—it's GOD calling.

Will you call Him back?

Chapter 11

When the Enemy Starts Interfering with GOD's Calls

The enemy knows when we are getting enough of this world, and that spiritual hunger we are born with begins to rise.

And he also knows that only GOD, our Holy Father, through His Begotten Son, JESUS, can truly satisfy that hunger.

"Jesus answered, 'I am the way and the truth and the life. No one comes to the Father except through Me.'"
— John 14:6 (NIV)

The enemy sees that light sparking in the darkness he led us into.

He wants to extinguish it as soon as possible because ...

That little light, when ignited by GOD, becomes a consuming fire.

"For our God is a consuming fire." — Hebrews 12:29 (NIV)

As my repentance and spiritual hunger began to rise, the enemy started interfering with GOD's calls.

I began asking out loud—not directly to GOD—how I could fill this hunger.

And the enemy answered, saying...

"Worship the universe and yourself, anything but GOD."

He cannot tell us to worship him directly—that would be too obvious.

Instead, he uses fear and misconceptions about GOD to keep us from turning to Him.

We fear GOD because of what we think He cares most about—rules, punishment, judgment, restrictions—so the enemy fills the spiritual hunger with his counterfeit food:

Crystals, manifestation, yoga, astrology, tarot cards, energy healing, Law of Attraction, occult practices, divination, self-help gurus, self-worship, reincarnation, false idols, new age spirituality, and even the worship of things like nature, the universe, people, careers, and relationships—anything *except* GOD Himself.

And I fell for it.

Why?

Because these things do work… but only like worldly things.

They feel good at first, but they never fully satisfy.

You need more and more, but "more" is never enough.

These practices are like fast food for the mind, body, and soul:

They taste great and fill you temporarily, but they lack real nutrients.

They are easily accessible, but over time, they cause spiritual malnourishment.

They may seem trendy and appealing, but they bring long-term destruction.

Instead of connecting us to the true source—GOD— they subtly lead us away through counterfeits.

And I couldn't tell the difference ...

So, I started worshipping the universe and myself.

If I'm honest with you, it's hard not to when you don't have someone to guide you to GOD without triggering the fears and lies you've been told about Him.

My mom tried to lead me, but I was too triggered to listen.

And these things felt good.

They gave me a false sense of peace. But looking back, I now see they were just distractions.

They were like empty calories—they were momentarily satisfying but left me starving for more.

And—big AND—

They opened the door to spiritual deception—the enemy's realm.

How do I know?

Because before I turned to those things, my life looked more stable—but I was still lost. I wasn't facing emotional and mental turmoil. I hadn't yet been pulled into deep emotional spiritual confusion. On the surface, I was functioning. But underneath, I was spiritually asleep. I was chasing success, ignoring my pain, and unknowingly drifting further from GOD.

It wasn't until I opened the door to other spiritual paths through these practices I mentioned before that the darkness became undeniable:

- Emotional and mental turmoil

- Panic attacks and unexplained anxiety

- Spiritual confusion and nightmares

- Addictions I couldn't shake

- Distance from the people who loved me most

- Shame and guilt I couldn't explain

- Bursts of anger and waves of depression

I thought I was seeking peace... but I was welcoming destruction.

Looking back, it all began when I turned to those false spiritual paths.

Again, at first, these practices gave me what I was craving: peace, love, and clarity.

But when life hit me hard, the true fruits of these practices were exposed.

Instead of GOD's peace, they led to:

· Sexual immorality

· Impurity and debauchery

· Idolatry and witchcraft

· Hatred, discord, and jealousy

· Fits of rage and selfish ambition

· Dissensions, factions, and envy

"The acts of the flesh are obvious: sexual immorality, impurity and debauchery; idolatry and witchcraft; hatred, discord, jealousy, fits of rage, selfish ambition, dissensions, factions and envy; drunkenness, orgies, and the like. I warn you, as I did before, that those who live like this will not inherit the kingdom of God." — *Galatians 5:19–21 (NIV)*

Why?

Because they are counterfeits.

They only work for a time—or until you reach a deeper spiritual level.

But GOD is eternal.

There is no time or space barrier to His provision, which is why only He can truly satisfy.

"Then Jesus declared, 'I am the bread of life. Whoever comes to Me will never go hungry, and whoever believes in Me will never be thirsty.'" — John 6:35 (NIV)

The enemy knows that once you taste GOD's food—His love, His Word, His promises—there's no turning back.

So, he will do everything to interfere with GOD's calls, because those calls will change your life.

Don't be deceived by his counterfeits.

If your life is bearing the enemy's fruits — sexual immorality, impurity, wild indulgence, idolatry, witchcraft, hatred, division, jealousy, outbursts of rage, selfish ambition, envy, drunkenness —

then hear me clearly: the enemy has cut your line.

But when your life is directed by GOD, our Holy Father, through our Lord and Savior Jesus, your life will reflect His fruits:

- Love

- Joy

- Peace

- Patience

- Kindness

- Goodness

- Faithfulness

- Gentleness

- Self-control

No matter what happens in your life.

"But the fruit of the Spirit is love, joy, peace, forbearance, kindness, goodness, faithfulness, gentleness and self-control. Against such things there is no law."
— *Galatians 5:22–23 (NIV)*

Take a moment. Look at the fruit in your life. What is it telling you?

Has the enemy cut your line to GOD?

If so, it's not too late to reclaim it.

Block the lies.
Break the patterns.

And call Him back.

GOD has been waiting.

Chapter 12

The Moment I Called GOD Back

It was in the middle of a relationship—when peace turned to torment and light to darkness—that I realized the enemy had his arms around me.

How did I know?

Because my life was suddenly filled with verbal and physical abuse, addictions, spiritual darkness, and division—something I had never experienced before.

NEVER.

I was blessed to grow up in a family and have had relationships where respect was foundational. We had our struggles, of course—insecurities, misunderstandings, and moments of passive-aggressiveness—but it never escalated to the level of destruction I was now facing.

So how did it get there?

That relationship I had with someone, once built on peace and love, had been corrupted by spiritual counterfeits and sinful living. The very things I had turned to for comfort and peace—new age meditation, self-help, energy healing, even seemingly innocent spiritual practices—only opened spiritual doors I didn't know existed. And when combined with an unrepentant life—sex outside of marriage, lies, manipulation, porn—I unknowingly gave the enemy permission to wreak havoc in my soul and in that relationship.

Satan was destroying me from within—one compromise at a time—while I thought I was just "healing" or "finding myself."

The truth? I was being deceived.

And it was only when the pain outweighed the illusion, that my soul craved something real.

And GOD knew it.

But He also knew I couldn't call Him.

Because I had allowed the enemy into my life without knowing.

So, GOD did what He does best—He loved me.

He saw that I was lost, trapped, and deceived. He knew my heart better than I did. He knew I didn't truly want this path, that I was grasping at illusions out of desperation. And because of that, He intervened.

Why would He intervene if He respects my free will?

Because He saw what I couldn't. He saw where I was headed—toward destruction and death. He knew I didn't want the deception anymore. He knew I longed for truth, even if I didn't know how to ask for it.

"What do you think? If a man owns a hundred sheep, and one of them wanders away, will he not leave the ninety-nine on the hills and go to look for the one that wandered off? And if he finds it, truly I tell you, he is happier about that one sheep than about the ninety-nine that did not wander off. In the same way, your Father in heaven is not willing that any of these little ones should perish." — Matthew 18:12–14 (NIV)

GOD chased after me, His lost sheep.

How did He intervene?

Through hardships in that relationship...

Sometimes, love comes in the form of separation.

And now I see that His way was far better than the path I was on.

Imagine cutting yourself deeply with a knife. You have two choices: you can endure the discomfort of getting stitches so the wound can heal properly, or you can let it bleed, hoping it will heal on its own. If you choose the latter, the pain lingers longer, the wound stays open, and the scar left behind is far worse.

He's the greatest surgeon, and His healing is miraculous.

So He separated me from what was harming me. He stripped away everything that wasn't of Him.

And suddenly, I had nowhere else to turn.

The worldly pleasures and spiritual counterfeits that once distracted me had lost their power. And in that moment of desperation, the impact of my mother's intercessory prayers began to break through.

Amazing.

Those prayers—prayers that seemed unanswered for years—started softening my heart and tuning my spirit back to Him.

It was like static slowly clearing from a radio signal. For the first time in a long time… I could hear Him.

So, I finally called Him back.

I remember falling to my knees during one of those hardships and crying out:

"GOD, if You really exist, please reveal Yourself to me. What do I do?"

I remember that moment like it was yesterday.

Later that day, I went to my usual coffee shop while in Porto, Portugal. I sat there, lost in my thoughts, when a song started playing faintly in the background. The melody was unfamiliar, but the lyrics caught my attention.

I got up and walked toward the speaker to hear it more clearly. And then, I heard these words:

"When I find myself in times of trouble,
Mother Mary comes to me,
Speaking words of wisdom, let it be..."

I grabbed my phone and used Shazam to find out the name of the song.

And in that moment, I knew.

I recognized His Voice.

I recognized His Love.

I recognized His Spirit.

I recognized His Presence.

He told me, *Let it be.*

It was Him.

Answering my call.

Telling me what to do.

Revealing Himself to me in the simplest yet most profound way.

"Trust in the Lord with all your heart and lean not on your own understanding; in all your ways submit to Him, and He will make your paths straight." — *Proverbs 3:5–6 (NIV)*

I was overwhelmed. I hurried back to my Airbnb, and as soon as I walked through the door, I collapsed on the floor in tears. But these weren't ordinary tears.

I wept. Deep, soul-cleansing weeping.

And it felt so good.

I felt seen. I felt heard. I felt safe. I felt loved.

I felt nourished in a way I had never experienced before.

I wept for hours, thanking GOD for revealing Himself to me, for answering my call.

At that moment, I knew without a doubt that GOD existed.

There was no universe without Him.
There was no *me* without Him.
There was nothing without Him.

I accepted Him as my Creator.

No more counterfeits.

No more running.

That was the moment everything started to change.

But truthfully...

I had no idea how deeply He was about to move in my life.

That call was just the beginning.

Chapter 13

The Missing Piece After Our Relationship Started

It's easy to feel GOD's love when we're at our lowest points—when we seek Him.

Why?

Because if we seek Him wholeheartedly, He will not abandon us. He loves us too much to do that.

"But if from there you seek the Lord your God, you will find Him if you seek Him with all your heart and with all your soul." — Deuteronomy 4:29 (NIV)

His love, peace, and comfort are so evident in our moments of need.

But here's the truth: we don't just want to experience His love and peace in those difficult moments.

We want to feel Him all the time.

Imagine feeling that love, peace, and clarity constantly. Doesn't it sound amazing?

Well, that level of connection with GOD requires effort, just like any relationship. But, more importantly, it requires that we accept His Only Begotten Son, Jesus Christ, as our Lord and Savior—not just GOD as our Creator.

"Jesus said to him, 'I am the way, the truth, and the life. No one comes to the Father except through Me.'"
— John 14:6 (NKJV)

Here's the truth:

Without Jesus, GOD is simply our Creator.

He is our GOD, yes, but without accepting Jesus as His Only Begotten Son, GOD is not our Holy Father yet.

And in order to have a real and true relationship with GOD as our Father, we need to embrace the image He created of His beloved Son as the foundation of our identity—our sonship and daughtership.

Without Jesus, the relationship is missing something crucial:

The adoption made possible through His Beloved Son.

"But when the set time had fully come, God sent His Son, born of a woman, born under the law, to redeem those under the law, that we might receive adoption to sonship." — Galatians 4:4–5 (NIV)

There came a point in my own walk with GOD where I needed to accept this truth. Despite experiencing GOD's love, I realized there was something deeper I had to connect with...

That something was Jesus.

I had known of Jesus all my life, but I always thought of Him as just a man—or maybe even a prophet—not as GOD's Only Begotten Son. I certainly didn't see Him as my Lord and Savior.

If I'm being honest, there was a part of me—my prideful, human side, influenced by spiritual deception—
that resisted accepting Jesus in that role. I couldn't understand how He, a man of flesh and blood like me, could be so different from other spiritual leaders like Buddha or others.

How could another man be my Savior? Shouldn't I be my own savior?

But GOD knew my thoughts, and there's nothing we can hide from Him.

He understood my hesitations, my resistance, and the confusion the enemy had wrapped me in.

"For the Lord searches every heart and understands every desire and every thought."
— *1 Chronicles 28:9 (NIV)*

He knew that accepting Him as Creator was the first step—but He also knew that for me to fully establish a relationship with Him the way He intended, I needed to accept Jesus as my Lord and Savior. And I needed time. I needed more understanding.

GOD, in His infinite love, was patient with me.

He understands that we all walk our spiritual journeys in unique ways, and He knew I would come to that revelation in His perfect time.

He would extend that gift to me whenever He knew I would be ready.

That time came through a series of life experiences, ones that GOD led me through, in order to show me that the missing piece of my relationship with Him was Jesus.

While writing *Are You Ignoring GOD's Calls?* GOD made it clear that I wasn't meant to share how I came to accept Jesus—at least not yet. And He gave me two specific reasons why:

(1) It would be too much information for the people He wanted to reach through me to digest, so He told me to write first about HIM in a concise, honest, and intentional way, and then write in a different book about Jesus.

(2) I still needed time to reflect and understand how I had ignored Jesus, even after accepting GOD in my life.

That's why I decided to wait to write the sequel, *Are You Ignoring Jesus?*

In this next book, I'll share how GOD guided me to accept Jesus as His Only Begotten Son and as my Lord and Savior. I'll reveal the steps of my journey and the lessons I learned along the way.

Because truthfully, a lot of what I went through between accepting GOD and accepting Jesus could have been avoided if I had just heard someone's testimony that truly resonated with me.

That's why GOD has called me to share my story, because He doesn't want His children to go through the same confusion and pain I did.

He doesn't want them to suffer through the hurt I caused and endured during that space between accepting GOD and truly accepting Jesus.

As you've read this book, if GOD has revealed to you the importance of accepting Him as your Creator, and your heart is stirring with the desire to know Jesus as your Lord and Savior, but the sequel isn't out yet, please don't wait.

You don't have to wait for a book, or for me. You can reach out to me anytime; I'd be honored to walk with you in that next step. But even more important, you can pray right now. GOD is ready to receive you.

My calling as GOD's disciple is to serve—however, whenever, and wherever He leads.

This isn't about selling books.

This is about expanding GOD's Kingdom—because He is worthy.

He is building it, even now. And He will continue until the end.

Helping one more son or daughter draw closer to Him is exactly what He wants from each of us.

Let me remind you again—GOD loves you.

And Jesus loves you too.

He is waiting for you. Not to judge you. Not to shame you.

But to free you…

"So if the Son sets you free, you will be free indeed."
—John 8:36 (NIV)

And to walk with you, redeem you, and love you like only He can.

If today you feel the stirring to accept Jesus as your Lord and Savior, you don't have to wait. You can pray right now, in your own words, or simply say this from your heart:

Jesus, I believe You are the Son of GOD.

I believe You died for my sins and rose again.

I confess that I need You, and I want to accept You into my heart.

Be my Savior. Be my Lord.

Help me walk in Your truth and grow in my relationship with You.

You gave Your life for my sins, so I give You mine.

Amen.

Notes of Encouragement

(The Call You Can Answer Right Now)

If you've made it this far, I believe with all my heart that it's not by accident.

GOD's been calling you.

Maybe you didn't recognize it at first. Maybe you've been running. Or maybe you've been quietly hoping He would reach out again—just one more time.

In a way that was undeniable.

Well… this is it.
The call you've been waiting for is ringing right now.

And the best part?

You don't have to be perfect to answer.
You don't need to have all the right words.
You don't need to fix everything before you come to Him.

He's not asking for perfection.
He's asking for permission—to move into your life, fill your heart, and lead you into the purpose you were created for.

If you haven't accepted GOD as your Creator and Heavenly Father and you've felt Him tugging on your heart during this book... don't wait.

That step is the one that changes *everything*.

Accepting GOD is the start of an infinite relationship that will bring a form of peace, love, and healing you have not felt to date.

You can say yes right now. You don't need to be part of a church or wait for the perfect time.

This is your moment.

Your moment to stop running.
Your moment to stop filling the void with things that never last.
Your moment to say: "I believe You exist. I want to know You. I want You in my life."

Or even to say "I'm not sure if You're real, but if You are, please reveal Yourself to me."

Just be honest. That's what GOD wants most—your heart, fully surrendered.

He is not asking you to have all the answers.
He's asking you to stop ignoring Him so He can show you who He is.

You don't need perfect words.
You just need a willing heart.

If you don't know where to start, here's a simple prayer you can say. Not magic words—just real ones. From your heart to His:

A Prayer to Answer the Call:

GOD,
I believe You're calling me.
I believe You created me for a reason,
and I want to know You.
I'm tired of running.
I'm tired of trying to do this alone.
I give You permission to come into my life.
Show me who You are.
Help me hear Your voice.
Teach me how to walk with You.
I may not understand everything right now,
but I want to start.
I want to answer Your call.
Amen.

If you prayed that prayer—or even if you didn't but feel something stirring—I just want to say: I'm proud of you.

You are not alone.
You are deeply loved.
And you've just made the most important decision of your life.

Welcome to the beginning of everything.

It only gets better from here.

And when you're ready to take the next step, you'll discover what I did—

that accepting GOD wasn't the end...

it was just the beginning.

Acknowledgments

First and most importantly, I want to thank my Lord and Savior, **Jesus Christ**.
Not only for guiding me and giving me the wisdom to write this book, but for giving me the greatest gift I have ever received—**His salvation**.

Writing this book helped me understand You better.
Writing this book helped me trust You more.
Writing this book helped me lean more on You.
Writing this book opened my heart to You.
Writing this book helped me see my brokenness.
Writing this book revealed how faithful and merciful You have always been.
Writing this book proved that with You, nothing is impossible.
Writing this book... drew me closer to You.

I also want to thank everyone who has been part of my life in one way or another—**family, partners, friends, mentors**, and even those who challenged me. Through each of you, GOD found a way to bring me closer to Him.

To anyone I may have ever hurt or wronged, knowingly or unknowingly—I am deeply sorry. My hope is that through GOD's grace, you can forgive me as He has forgiven me.

To Justin, my editor—whom the Lord GOD unexpectedly placed in my path to guide me through the editing and publishing process—and to Gustavo, my designer, whose creativity and heart helped bring this book to life visually, thank you both. And to all those who read early drafts and offered feedback, even those who are not believers yet, I'm deeply grateful. Each of you played a part in shaping this work and helping it reach those GOD intends to touch through it.

Lastly, to those reading this book: thank you for opening your heart. I pray that these words help you hear His voice more clearly, and that through my story, you recognize that GOD has been calling you too—all along.

**All glory to GOD, forever and ever.
Holy, Holy, Holy is GOD Almighty!**

About the Author

Jose Miguel Azares is a Canadian entrepreneur, author, and follower of Jesus Christ, originally from Venezuela. He came to Canada to pursue his Master's in Building Engineering at Concordia University and began his career at **Suncor Energy**, where he worked in civil engineering and project management.

After completing his **MBA at McGill University**, Jose transitioned into entrepreneurship—building ventures that merged creativity, technology, and human purpose.

He founded two successful startups: **REGRUB**, a boutique burger restaurant brand in Calgary known for its playful, creative, and community-driven spirit, and **NIDUM**, an immersive technology company serving high employee-turnover industries through innovative training solutions. His leadership earned him distinctions such as t**he DEAM (Disability Employment Awareness Month) Employer Award** and the **IDA (Distinguished Immigrant Award)** in Entrepreneurship and Innovation from the City of Calgary.

But after years of chasing worldly success and fulfillment through business ventures, achievements, and relationships, Jose came face to face with the emptiness that comes from living without spiritual direction.

That encounter marked the beginning of a deep and transformative journey back to his Creator.

Behind every accomplishment, he had been wrestling with a deeper longing—a purpose that success could never satisfy. It was only when he stopped ignoring GOD's call and surrendered his life to Christ that true transformation began. On **September 27, 2024**, Jose became a new follower of Christ, answering the call that changed everything.

In *Are You Ignoring GOD's Calls?*, Jose shares his raw and personal story—one filled with brokenness, repentance, and redemption—to help others recognize how GOD calls each of us into a real, personal relationship with Him. His message is simple but urgent: **GOD is calling, and every call has a purpose.**

Today, Jose identifies first and foremost as a **son of GOD and follower of Jesus Christ**. He continues to use his creativity and entrepreneurial experience to serve—supporting his family's business, **Nature Sante**, and leading faith-driven projects that reflect GOD's love, purpose, and truth.

He hopes this book inspires readers to stop running, listen to GOD's voice, and answer the call that changes everything!

.

www.ingramcontent.com/pod-product-compliance
Lightning Source LLC
LaVergne TN
LVHW041322080426
835513LV00008B/553